Roy King offers the strategic insight deliver. Drawing from a wealth of personal experience, careful study, and seasoned mentoring, this short book provides a 10,000 foot view of the life cycle and seasons every leader needs to understand in order to steward a church effectively through its mission. And while Roy is fully missional in his advice, he includes essentials that other writers often forget: the metastory of God's glory and the motivation of God's compassionate heart for people. *Helping a Church Live Well* will yield more applications per page than most; you will definitely want this in your library!

>JEROME DALEY
>Leadership Coach and Culture Consultant, Founder of Thrive9

Roy King has written a concise practical guide to understanding organizational life, with special focus on how it applies to local churches. Drawing on his extensive experience as a congregational consultant, Dr. King offers a strategy to help churches engage in an on-going process of walking with God as He builds His Church.

>DR. JOHN HARVEY
>Dean of the Seminary and School of Ministry, Columbia International University

What I appreciate about Roy King is his heart for Jesus Christ and His Church. His experiences in ministry and his gift of teaching shine through in this application of leadership principles and practices. Helping organizations understand their position in time, the areas that need to change, and how to lead through change brings hope and encouragement to the many challenging times we face. These principles and practices have been a great help to us at China Outreach Ministries.

>DR. GLEN OSBORN
>President, China Outreach Ministries

I have observed Roy consulting churches and organizations and coaching ministry leaders for several years. I believe God has used him in this service to provide perspective and encouragement. This book is another example of his heart for local churches to prosper as they see where they are and where God wants them to be.

>DR. BILL JONES
>President, Columbia International University

Helping the Church Live Well

Helping the CHURCH Live well

A Consultant's Approach to Assisting the Church

ROY KING

Columbia, South Carolina

Helping the Church Live Well: A Consultant's Approach to Assisting the Church

Copyright © 2015 by Roy King

LeaderSpace
317 S. Shields Road
Columbia, SC 29223
www.leaderspace.org

LeaderSpace provides resources to assist leaders in their personal development and to equip them for developing other leaders. This includes one-on-one leadership coaching, church consulting, and teaching in organizational and academic settings.

Cover and interior book design by Kelly Smith, Tallgrass Media.

Cover image by Filip Ologeanu. Used by permission.

Scripture quotations are from The Holy Bible, English Standard Version®, copyright © 2001 by Crossway Bibles, a publishing ministry of Good News Publishers. Used by permission. All rights reserved.

All rights reserved.
No part of this book may be reproduced in any form or by any electronic or mechanical means including information storage and retrieval systems, without permission in writing from the author. The only exception is for short excerpts quoted in a book review.

ISBN-13: 978-1-5174-7939-8

Contents

1	Introduction
7	Chapter 1 – Defining the Stages of Organizational Life
13	Chapter 2 – The Significance of Organizational Life Stages
19	Chapter 3 – The Life Cycle Is a Fact of Life & Death
29	Chapter 4 – The Symptoms of a Declining, Unhealthy Organization
39	Chapter 5 – Practices of Vibrant & Effective Organizations
57	Chapter 6 – The Importance of Seeing the Seasons of a Work Cycle
69	Conclusion – Suggestions on How to Lead
73	A Prayer for Leaders
75	Resources
77	Notes

Dedication

I dedicate this book to Dr. Gerald Parker. Gerald had a long and distinguished career in reading education at Appalachian State University in Boone, North Carolina and still resides there. In the "second half" of life he and his faithful partner, sidekick and loving wife, Mary, have had very fruitful disciple making ministry in China, Ukraine, and Russia. The travels have lessened with age, but many of Gerald's breakfasts and lunches are booked with men eager to receive his encouragement and to welcome his questioning mind. For years he has carried 3x5 cards in his pockets. The cards often contain a verse of Scripture for the week's mediation and prayer requests, but they also carry a list of men he seeks to befriend and spend time with on a regular basis. It is an honor for me to be on that list.

Gerald has been a friend, mentor, guide and support from 1975 right up to today. I would say that next to my wife Gerald is my best friend. He has the courage to ask the hard questions which prompt me to grow. He has the wisdom to understand the intentional, rigorous, time consuming process that true learning requires in order to change behavior and transform character. Gerald is never willing to settle for just throwing information at people without assisting them in practice and integration that also results in them passing that learning on to others.

Gerald is a trainer of trainers. Whether it is training those who teach reading or those who are making disciples of Jesus, his approach involves strategies, questions, guided experiences and evaluation to mine those experiences for growth. It would not be unusual for a given week to include a Skype visit to help me with a seminary course design, a strategy consultation with the director of an alcohol and drug rehab program, a time of encouragement with a friend who faces chronic challenges some would label mental illness, taking the time to befriend a prodigal running from Jesus but open to Gerald's love and challenges, and comforting one of the older widows in the church with Mary at his side.

Perhaps the biggest lesson Gerald has taught me is to walk in humility and embrace my own weakness. I have lost count of the number of times he has asked me, "So, Roy out of all the knowledge in the universe how much do you have about... (FILL IN THE BLANK with a person, situation, or judgment I am making)?" Gerald would be the first to admit he has many flaws and weaknesses. He can list several of them easily because he is frequently asking God to cover them with his abundant grace and mercy. And He has. Gerald's humility and awareness of his own areas of growth keep him learning from his students. He refuses to accept that he is my teacher and instead insists I am his. I bet he does that with all of his students. Gerald, I am spending my life being your student and I plan to never finish your class.

Roy King
August 2015

Acknowledgments

This book would not have come about without the support of Dr. John Harvey in my study leave for the spring semester of 2015. Thank you for being willing to add to your load so you could lighten mine and free me to think in fresh ways about material I have been using in consulting for the past 18 years.

I am also aware of how my wife, Pandora, took on some of my household chores and let me sit in my office—which I call my cave—and tune out the world to live in my ideas and words. For over 40 years she has believed God had given me something to say and has poured courage into me to trust God and step out and say it.

God arranged the schedule of one of my former students, Kelly Smith, and his wife Joice, to be in Columbia this year so he could design the cover, Joice could edit, and Kelly could then lay out the text and get this work into print and e-publication. Kelly and Joice have helped make this book more readable and are responsible for bringing it from my computer to the world. Contact Kelly at Tallgrass Media (www.tallgrassmedia.com) for help with your projects!

Introduction

Perspective is Critical to Effective Leadership

Dr. Robert Clinton, professor of leadership at Fuller Theological Seminary for many years, says that leadership is all about *perspective*. The better the perspective, the better the leadership contribution will be.[1] Perspective is a way of seeing. Godly perspective sees people, events and circumstances as God sees them and then responds in alignment to his vision. Jesus rebuked people for their lack of perspective. They had eyes but failed to see. They had ears but failed to hear. Echoing the prophets of the Old Testament this kind of blindness and deafness was the result of hearts that had drifted into a pride filled attempt to walk with God on their own terms.

In my own spiritual journey God has made Perspective 101 a required class which I have had to repeat several times! His Spirit, using the Bible and close advisors, has often challenged my vision and corrected my perspective. During one of my children's teenage years I was struggling with knowing how to love well in a season of rebellion. God's correction came through a friend who challenged me to go home and to go through the photo albums of our child's life with my wife. He encouraged us by saying, "See your child as more than the problems resulting from the bad choices of the present. See the whole person who God loves and Jesus died to redeem." That one shift in our vision fueled the proper kind of love we needed to offer at that time.[2]

When I began coaching church and ministry leaders, one of my first clients had already served in three churches in less than ten years and was struggling in the fourth. His perspective was, "These people are the problem. They do not want to change. The leaders told me they wanted change but once I was here and started leading us into change they resisted me." The story was basically the same for all four congregations. He had a difficult time receiving my counsel. As a matter of fact, it was the last conversation we had. I am confident there was some truth in his perspective of the resistance to change by the people, but when I suggested that perhaps his leadership was a significant part of the problem, my perspective clashed with his own vision. Letting go of self-justification is like never eating dessert again. Why would a person let go of something that makes them feel so good and righteous in their anger, hurt and resentment?

A leader's perspective shows up in all aspects of life. In our first home I went wild with my trimmers and cut my azalea bushes back away from the windows. But because of *when* I did it, I guaranteed they would not bloom the next season. I was performing the correct task but did not have a correct perspective of the flowering cycle. My choice, made with good intentions, had a negative impact.

In the pages that follow, I am asking you to examine your current understanding of the church or organization you lead and hold it up to God, asking him to correct your perspective. I am also asking you to take your view of daily work and to be willing to exchange it for God's view. The Bible calls that repentance. Repentance is not just for starting our relationship as a Jesus follower, it is also the primary means we move toward maturity in Christ as his followers and are qualified to serve as leaders in his name.

INTRODUCTION TO LIFE CYCLE AND SEASONS

Leaders make better decisions when they have a perspective that aligns with God's will. They become more effective in solving problems, resolving challenges, and seizing opportunities. They love God and others better! They also reduce the damage they do to people within their influence.

In this book, I will be examining two facets of perspective: the stages of the organizational life cycle and the seasons of fruitful work.

THE LIFE CYCLE

The Life Cycle is best viewed as the entire birth to death experience of an organization. I will use the term 'organization' to cover both congregational and parachurch ministry structures. Since we can never know the future with certainty, we can only determine where we are in a life cycle by comparing the present to the past and to what is expected.

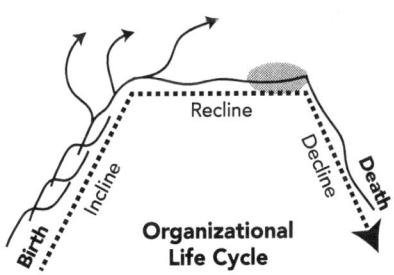

Examples of Life Cycle

1. A church formed in the 1950s in a rural part of the county. But by the 1990s, urban sprawl transformed many of the smaller farms into subdivisions and shopping plazas. The church continues to be led by many of the families who own farms or those who

sold out and moved further away but drive back for services. The church has been stable in attendance but is aging. There are very few newer residents in the church.

2. A mission agency was birthed by a visionary evangelistic leader and has expanded for the past 50 years. The leader died a few years ago and the organization is facing tremendous challenges with technology, mobility and the needs of missionary children. Many insiders express privately that they feel most of the field workers are independent operators just using the home base to park funds for support and projects they create. There are no longer any unified objectives for the organization as a community.

SEASONS

Seasons define a shorter term cycle for specific projects, events and activities of ministry. There are many seasons in the life cycle of an organization, just as there are many seasons during the life of an apple tree. Seasons will look somewhat different based on the stage of development in the life cycle.

SEASONAL CYCLE OF FRUITFUL WORK

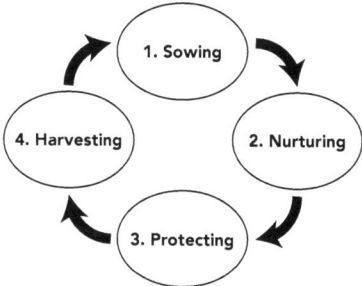

Examples of Seasons

1. A church starts a daycare and after school program so the facility is getting more use during the week and to meet needs in the community. The director and the staff are fine people but are not part of the hosting congregation. Is this headed for a harvest season of fruitful ministry?

2. A ministry offers three-week summer mission projects, and operates summer camps in the USA and three overseas. Leaders are trying to create a way to effectively communicate with and recruit young people to help lead the ministry. How will the leaders design seasonal stages of a project to address this challenge?

USING THE LIFE CYCLE AND SEASONS

Several important leadership questions shape a leader's perspective:

- *Why* does this organization exist?
- *What* are the desired results or outcomes of the organization?
- *How* will the organization be structured to assist the people in accomplishing the results?
- *Who* will have authority and responsibility for investing the resources of the organization (resources = time, money, facilities, equipment)?
- *When* will the leaders take the next round of necessary actions?

This is not an exhaustive list and perhaps you can add ones that fit your context as your read the book.

In this book we focus on two of these important leadership questions:

- *Where* is the organization in its stage of life?
- *What* kind of work is most needed to make the current efforts potentially fruitful?

Life Cycle theory is a tool to assist us in getting perspective on the *where* question. Seasons is a template for thinking through effective ministry tactical plans to help answer the *what* question.

THINKING THROUGH:

1. How could you be more aware to the role your perspective contributes to your attitudes, actions and words?
2. What do you already know from prior learning or experience about stages in a life cycle or seasonal stages of fruitful work?

Chapter 1

Defining the Stages of Organizational Life

The life cycle is a tool to help leaders understand where an organization is in its journey of development and decline. Life cycle theory helps leaders answer the question, "Where are we living right now?" As I coach congregational and parachurch ministry leaders, I have observed many poor strategic decisions being made by leaders who fail to consider the life stage of the organization.

Examples

A young pastor serving his first congregation feels that he has all of the answers for what a healthy effective congregation should be and do. He has read all of the books his seminary professors suggested and he has all of the answers. His vision was to turn the church into the next "Saddleback". Even though it took Rick Warren over 20 years of labor in a church plant before he had made enough mistakes (and successes) to write *The Purpose Driven Church,* this young leader plans to knock it out in two years, three at the most! But he fails to account for how leading a seventy-five year old congregation in a declining small town will impact the approach to change. He ignores the aspect of Rick's journey of how he started a church plant in a fast-growing, unchurched and high-population density area. I think you can probably see the light at the end of this particular ministry tunnel—and it is not sunlight—it is the train!

Ministry leaders love to get together and glean leadership principles, practices, and models from the most successful ones in the room. Then the leaders scatter to their diverse ministry settings and seek to apply these world-changing new examples without carefully considering the organizational life stage where they live. This is often not only ineffective, but can also be destructive. After a few cycles of adrenaline rush at a conference, and returning home with a new notebook, only to see little significant change, these leaders arrive at the conclusion that the problem is the conference setting. They become cynical and hardened to going to more events. When leaders ignore the reality of the setting where God has placed them, they risk squandering their leadership influence and speeding the decay of the organization.

> When leaders ignore the reality of the setting where God has placed them, they risk squandering their leadership influence and speeding the decay of the organization.

LIFE CYCLE STAGES

Those who have written on life cycle theory divide the life cycle into various stages and use various terms to label the stages. To provide a foundational overview I have chosen three major stages with some specification within them.

Incline – Includes 1. Birth, 2. Early Childhood, 3. Adolescence, and 4. Early Adulthood (This represents approximately 15% of congregations in the United States).

Recline or Plateau – Includes 5. Mature Adulthood and 6. Midlife, (often involving a midlife crisis). (This represents approximately 60% of congregations in the United States).

Decline – Includes 7. Early Aging (think AARP), Late Decline (think assisted living) and 8. Death (think Hospice). (Represents approximately 25% of congregations in the United States).[3]

The percentages listed above should set a leader's perspective toward what it will require to lead an organization in the incline stage. The leader in an inclining church must accept that he or she will be in the minority and must lead differently from the 80%. I believe the same perspective would apply to any non-profit organization.[4] Leaders who duplicate the majority strategy, when the majority are in recline or decline, are not choosing a wise course.

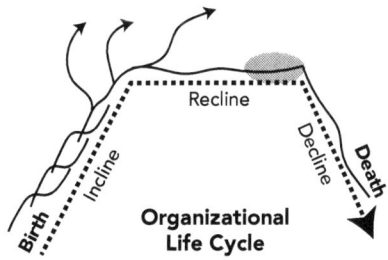

ORGANIZATIONAL STAGES

Some consultants serving non-profit organizations use five stages which describe the unique consulting and coaching questions that tend to surface for a stage of development or decline.

1. *Birthing* is the fragile beginning with many threats to survival. Questions leaders ask are about assembling people and financial resources and what to do first.

2. *Resourcing* stage organizations are growing and are asking resource investment questions. What are staffing and priority infrastructure needs? How do we identify, train, launch and coach enough new leaders to keep up? This stage will also include those organizations seeking to be a resource to other organizations.

3. *Refocusing* organizations are at a plateau stage and/or early decline. They still have leaders around but they are aware that

while there is the appearance of stability, they are aging and subtle shifts are occurring that cause concern.

4. *Restoring* organizations are in late decline. They are losing leaders or potential leaders and other resources are also evaporating. There are a storm of negative challenges gathering which are usually perceived as crises threatening survival. These organizations may become open to outside help but often cannot afford to pay for what they need.

5. *Replanting/Rebirthing* organizations are at or near death. They face taking the remains of the organization and prayerfully investing them to birth new organizations, or in supporting vibrant and effective organizations with whom they share a common purpose.

CONCLUSION

Unless organizations are built to be flexible and are adept at processing change, they become static. The reality is that the world IS changing. And one of the major ways it is changing is in the approaches to creating relational connections and in forging community. This shift in the *how* of relationships is very important to ministry-purposed organizations. If ministry organizations look like a home furnished in the 60s they are no longer seen as relevant and limit their capacity to wield influence.

THINKING THROUGH:

1. What is an example in your life where having the wrong perspective, even if you had good motives, produced little or even negative results?
2. How would you hold up your perspective to the Lord and invite

his Spirit to bring your vision into alignment with how God sees the place he has assigned you?

3. Draw a picture in the space below that might describe the particular life cycle stage of your church or organization.

Chapter 2

The Significance of Organizational Life Stages

Life cycle theory rests on one simple assumption: that the life of an organization follows the same basic life cycle as biological life. Any man-made structure constructed for organizing people to accomplish tasks—whether a business, church, or parachurch agency—goes through distinct stages of life, moving through stages of development and decline from birth to death.

- *Forming*—Coming into existence. The organization is created, born, planted or launched. Most organizations are very fragile during this stage.
- *Growing and Maturing*—New growth and reproduction occur.
- *Aging*—The organization experiences a rate of decay. The rate of change varies a great deal among organizations.
- *Declining*—The organization becomes less effective, fruitful or productive, especially when measured against the amount of resources consumed in getting the intended results. More energy and resources are consumed on maintenance than on advancement and research and development.
- *Dying*—What is left over when the organization dies often becomes resources for new organizations.

In addition, all through the stages of the life cycle a person or an organization will face opposition. Attacks and threats to health are a normal part of life and come from both outside forces and internal forces malfunctioning. There will always be resistance to healthy growth.

THE WISDOM IN DISCERNING THE LIFE CYCLE STAGES

In many ways, leading within an organization parallels parenting. The apostle Paul had a perspective of leading the church as "parenting leadership".[5] Just as parents prioritize goals and ask different questions at each stage of a child's development, leaders need to make sure they understand the priority issues appropriate to the life stage of the organization.

A leadership proverb I use with every leader I coach or consult is, "Good leadership is much more about revisiting good questions over and over instead of a quest for the one perfect answer." I believe that good questions are *the* key to getting a better perspective and then making better decisions. I also believe it is rare to discover "one perfect answer" in a sin-damaged world.

When parents are watching over the child's development they ask two different types of questions:

Health questions—come from various measurements and assessments focusing on levels of energy, vitality, ability to learn, relational interaction and also seeking to detect symptoms of any illness or malfunction.

Growth questions—include assessments such as the child's height and weight, and are based on norms by level of development. Growth questions gather and assess in light of the stage of maturity. I would also include the more subjective assessment of family and friends who the child resembles in looks, personality and approach to life.

While parents may prioritize health over growth, there is a range of normative expectations for both. Poor health erodes growth potential. Normal growth may not indicate health. Recently a 15-year-old high school student died during a football practice. His growth was normal but his enlarged heart had gone undetected and shortened his life. Sound health normally produces a satisfactory rate of growth.

It may sound spiritual for church leaders to say, "We may be small but we are focused on depth and not compromising for shallow growth like some others." This holy remnant perspective is often discounting the lack of growth, and is masking illness and decay just below the surface. Yes, there are cases where a simple head count does not indicate the true growth in life changes taking place. A church among a people very resistant to the gospel, or one in an area where many people leave the geographic circle of the congregation, such as a resort area or a university town, must not compare themselves only to churches in stable communities and where there is a great openness among people to embracing the faith. But, it is normative to expect health to contribute to fruitful growth.

Health and growth are helpful categories but become less helpful if leaders of organizations shrink the definitions. We do this by considering only a few questions.

Here are some examples of assumptions we may make that indicate we aren't asking a breadth of good questions:

- We may assume that we are a healthy organization if there is no disruptive conflict consuming our leadership focus and energy.
- We may assume that we are growing if attendance at a large event or financial resources are increasing close to our expectations.

These shrunken definitions lead to leaders saying, "If it isn't broken, don't fix it." It becomes a way to avoid addressing concerns and making changes. While these considerations do have value they are only the tip of the iceberg.

So, I have adopted the terms *vibrant* and *effective*. Vibrance carries the image of alive joyful health that is much more than just absence of pain. Effectiveness assessment leads the group back to the reason the organization was formed and to evaluate the current performance against the intended purpose.

Vibrant and effective organizations will be on the front side of the life cycle for a much longer period of time. We will discuss how to extend the quality life of an organization later, but I would like to close this chapter with a word that I hope is encouraging. Christians believe God is sovereign over a person's days. Our ability to control our own destiny is limited. We may consistently engage in a healthy lifestyle and seek to listen to God and follow King Jesus each day into whatever assignments he offers. But, we cannot control the number of our days. As much as I enjoy time management tools and principles (I even wrote a book on it!) I cannot make my 24-hour day expand to 25 hours.

And which of you by being anxious can add a single hour to his span of life? If then you are not able to do as small a thing as that, why are you anxious about the rest? —Luke 12:25-26 (ESV)

There is something freeing in clarifying my responsibility. I am a manager, or a steward, but not the owner. I am a servant but never the master. I am free to accept my duties, including making choices and investing my leadership contribution as wisely as I can, but I must then leave the results in my Father's hands.

Come now, you who say, "Today or tomorrow we will go into such and such a town and spend a year there and trade and make a profit"— yet you do not know what tomorrow will bring. What is your life? For you are a mist that appears for a little time and then vanishes. Instead you ought to say, "If the Lord wills, we will live and do this or that." As it is, you boast in your arrogance. All such boasting is evil. So whoever knows the right thing to do and fails to do it, for him it is sin. —James 4:13-17 (ESV)

THINKING IT THROUGH:

1. Can you identify the life cycle stage that best describes the organization where you serve?
2. List the "health" and "growth" questions that leaders in the organization currently employ to conduct evaluation?
3. What are some questions to consider related to being vibrant and effective so leaders gain a more accurate perspective of the organization?

Chapter 3

The Life Cycle Is a Fact of Life & Death

There is no biblical or historical basis for the idea that our created structures are blessed with eternal life. If we admit a similarity between the God-imposed biological life cycle and organizational life cycle, it actually makes sense to believe that organizations created as a work of people's hands inherit the same limits as the people starting and running them.

Only individuals live beyond physical death in eternal life or death. Organizations do not travel beyond the grave. Even the kingdom of God which comes into full expression at Christ's return is a very different organization from the one Jesus introduced in Luke 17:21 as the kingdom of God within you. One's money stays on this side of the grave and it also true of the organizations it funds.

Spend time scanning through church history books and you will find denominational networks, congregations and many other types of ministry structures that were highly visible in their day but are now faded memories. There are "cemeteries" or "junk yards" filled with worn out, wrecked and close to dying, old-age organizations.

Doesn't it look foolish to see a 70 year-old man attempting to dress like a 25 year-old? The preoccupation with avoiding the appearance of getting old does little to change the impact of aging on our state of health and vigor. So, why do we often attempt to manage and envision an organization as if it has an unlimited life span? We cannot choose to avoid a personal life cycle and it is an inaccurate perspective to believe our organizations would be immune.

WOULD WE BUILD AND RUN OUR ORGANIZATIONS DIFFERENTLY IF THEY HAD AN EXPECTED TERMINAL POINT?

The five-year mission partnership into Russia known as "CoMission" and the "AD 2000 movement" are suggestive of models of organizations built around developing and advancing the overall mission of God's global work without leaving monuments of creaking, aging organizations consuming strategic resources for the next generation to sustain.

PEOPLE ARE MORE VALUABLE THAN THE ORGANIZATIONS THEY BUILD.

Structure and systems are the muscles, organs and skeleton of organization. These infrastructure elements emerge out of personal relationships and objectives. People, gathering around a mission and experiencing life in community, will stimulate the birth of a context; some kind of structure. Whether it is the Chinese home churches, Korean mega-churches, or denominational networks, the activities of people rallying around common purposes give birth to organizations.

The structures that emerge are inevitably colored by cultural definitions of power, responsibilities and economics and many other organizational forces. The unique cultural fingerprint of every organization is one reason the church has many varied shapes throughout church history and around the world. The organization has value serving as the "clothing" for the group. But we cannot equate the value of the organization to the individuals gathering to be a part of it.

We have greater freedom to experiment or tamper with organizational life than we should take with people. We can "abort", "euthanize", "attempt cloning", and engage in "genetic manipulation" of organizational structures which would be biblically challenged as being inappropriate for persons. We are not constrained by the biblical ethical concerns applying to every precious human life which bears God's image. Organizations bear *our* image not God's. There are few biblical principles or commands directed to how we organize ourselves.

Organizations are the boxes God gift wraps people in. People are the treasured gifts. Organizations are the containers for communities of disciples to reside in as they gather around a common mission.

People tend to ascribe value to organizations because of the cost and sacrifice invested to create and sustain them. They usually came into being through great sacrifices of sweat and blood, time and money. The facilities that are sometimes a part of the organization become the places of many good memories of our encounters with our God. Perhaps God gives organizations a limited shelf life to prevent them from becoming idols we treasure more than him.

> Organizations are the containers for communities of disciples to reside in as they gather around a common mission.

THE CONTRIBUTION AND DANGERS IN PLANNING

What can we discover about a wise perspective on planning? What do we learn when we reflect on how persons and organizations form and execute plans? A plan expresses intention. Plans say, "We intend to use our time and money in certain ways as we move into the future." We then use budget spreadsheets and calendars to track how the unfolding present reality conforms to our intention, our plan.

Knowing God's will and living life with him one day at a time for an individual is more like *walking* on a journey than *planning* with a blueprint.[6] "Whoever claims to live in him must walk as Jesus did." Most organizational planning processes are very different from going on a journey where God is the initiator and we are responding to his lead.

I have turned sixty. Yet I had to arrive at that mile marker one day at a time; 21,900 of them to be exact. Each of those days included thousands of steps, leading to hundreds of crossroads, and hundreds of choices. And each day placed me at a different point in my journey. Every one of those days I could say, "I am once again at a place I have never been before." This "new" place invites me to look around and approach each step in a childlike questioning learning mode. Daily, in my never-before-walked-path, I am discovering God's presence and power to respond to every person, event or circumstance he brings to me. Ministering to aging parents, adult children, and a seasoned marriage requires a fresh daily dose of God's grace.[7]

Christian organizations have spent millions of kingdom dollars on long-term planning, and from my perspective most of it is a waste. Much of our planning is a sad attempt to copy corporate models of planning. These models have a starting point that leaves no room for a dramatic intervention by God.

Our timelines, projections and budgets may even dull us to anticipating and hungering for him. Long-range planning is often an attempt to extend our very limited human control into the future and "play God". Jesus has clearly instructed us to invest in the future by how we live today. We are to always place our planning, in humility, under his sovereignty not seeking to project an appearance of our control of the future.[8]

> *Jesus has clearly instructed us to invest in the future by how we live today.*

CHRISTIAN ORGANIZATIONS DO NEED TO PLAN

Planning for Christians is reminding ourselves what God treasures and then committing to be intentional, regardless of the reaction of the world around us, to investing ourselves in bringing those gifts to him. And what does God treasure? The answer is people![9] A "treasure hunt" approach to planning engages those in the organization in a continual process of planning to walk with God today, as he is building his church instead of a static set of predictions and goals. A "walking with God" planning process will parallel the biblical principles of how an individual navigates the life cycle through seeking wisdom, seeing God's values and heart, clinging to God in faith-filled prayer and joining what he is doing.[10]

GOOD NEWS AND BAD NEWS ABOUT PLANNING

The "good news" is that a well-executed planning process opens our eyes to acknowledge reality and cuts through our denial of serious issues facing us. The Bible is filled with this kind of reality check and is always calling God's people to see themselves and their world as they really exist.

The "bad news" is that planning will always leave us with a sense of disappointment. In a fallen world a great deal of the dreams and desires found in our plans become just another notebook on the shelf. The planned point of destination and where we actually arrive will almost never match. And that can be discouraging. West Point teaches soldiers to always plan to replan the plan. The military capture the limit of planning with the phrase, "No plan survives contact with the enemy." Look at the research of how few college graduates end up working in the area of their college major. Or, examine some of the simpler plans in your life:

1. How did your plan for what you would accomplish for yesterday match what actually occurred?
2. Did you plan your last vacation? Did you read all of the books

you took with you? Did you go to all of the places? Did the rain cancel some of your plans?

We simply do not have as much control and influence over results as most planning guides imply. It is much better to focus on what God values, to walk with him daily, and to be honest about where he has placed you. Short term tactical plans that focus on immediate obedience are much more in line with biblical models.

GOD PROMPTS LEADERS TOWARD THE FUTURE

God's Spirit often gives leaders a perspective that the future needs to be different from the present. I recognize I am with a leader when they say things like:

1. "This is NOT right. We must do something." Notice that they do not just complain, but they also have a willingness to take action that will make a difference.
2. "I see so much wasted potential. I wake up praying we can get clarity and move out."
3. "I think what is being proposed may work but have we considered this new approach."

God's grace gifts leaders with the skills and creativity to propose what those improvements could be, and to initiate a plan describing how to bring them into reality. God stirs his people with a groaning (2 Corinthians 5, Romans 8) of longing for the sinful decay of this world to be replaced by its intended glory. God stirs up deep passion in his people for redemptive action. Salt and light intervention and justice-inspired compassionate sacrifices honor God and advance his mission. These biases to actions are elements of a normal walk by faith with him.

But, to sit down in a room with "outside experts" and the organizational leaders and mapping out a 3-to 10-year timeline plan for preserving and advancing the organization seems to be unwise effort. That approach to planning is often about as far from capturing the wind-like moving of the Spirit as a written program on Sunday morning can predict and orchestrate the worship God intends for his people to experience flowing from their hearts to his throne.

GOD DOES NOT GIVE US A GUARANTEE OF LONG LIFE.

There is a normative 70-year life cycle stated in the Bible for persons but it can be cut short by many different causes. People often ask me to put time frames on the stages of the organizational life cycle. I can't do it. You meet some individuals who at 75 years old are on the "incline" in terms of living with a sense of new beginnings and faith risks.

Life Cycle of a Vibrant and Effective 75 year old who lives to 90

You may also recall meeting a 25 year-old who has already reached serious "decline." Much of aging really is in the mind and heart and can be observed in individuals and organizations. I have met 90 year-olds who are learning new things and eager for God's next adventure. I have met lost-to-living 25 year-olds content to surf through life with their eyes buried in their social networks on their phone and their definition of an adventure is catching the latest movie.

> Much of aging really is in the mind and heart and can be observed in individuals and organizations.

Life Cycle of a 25 year old living in decline to 90

I see organizations with similar approaches to life. Some organizations may serve the people of God for just a brief window of time and yet leave a treasured historical legacy. Other organizations become like noisy machinery generating a great deal of activity but yielding very little valuable contribution for the majority of their life.

GOD'S SOVEREIGNTY INCLUDES OUR CREATED STRUCTURES.

Many times in the Bible God raises up leaders and casts down nations. God has various ways of touching our structures to accomplish his greater goal of freeing human hearts to a loving relationship under his rule.

Psalm 2 illustrates the futile attempts of kings and leaders to "rule" their organizations in rebellion against him. At the end of the Psalm the call goes to leaders to both bow and find refuge in his gracious rule. Many of Jesus' parables described in vivid terms how God deals with those who attempt to live apart from acknowledging their need for him.[11] God often uses forces outside of our organizations to either "shape" or "replace" our structures. Just ask Jeremiah! God has no problem sweeping our kingdoms into the dust bin to get our attention and bring us to him. This certainty of God's rule should color our perspective of planning and consider what God is doing to the life span of the organizations we lead.

ORGANIZATIONS ONLY HAVE VALUE TO THE DEGREE THEY SERVE GOD'S PEOPLE

One of the key indicators that an organization is in "decline" is when people feel in bondage to the organizational structure instead of empowered by it. People are pressured, often by the leaders, to sustain an organization even though it is no longer contributing effectively to the original mission.

Healthy structures are channels for empowering and engaging people. Unhealthy structures become like massive ticks—sucking resources, strength and focus from people. A proverb in adult education is that adult learners "vote with their feet." If the learner does not find the adult education class relevant to their learning goal they simply do not come back. Instead of expending great amounts of energy seeking to motivate people to attend the programs of the organization, perhaps leaders should ask, "Why are the people not motivated to commit to what we are offering?"

AN ORGANIZATION ONLY HAS VALUE TO THE DEGREE IT SERVES GOD'S PURPOSES.

Desire and passion motivates the choices made in building a life. In his book *Mere Christianity* C.S. Lewis says the problem is that many expressions of human desire are too small. We go for food, drink, and sex—because they are shadows of the real desire for God, heaven and glory.

Many organizations started as tools to propel people into God's kingdom adventure become museums within a few generations, filled with casual observers slowly filing past pictures portraying victories of days gone by. The desires of the people within the organization become too small. These shrunken objectives speed the decay of the organization. What a challenge it is to make sure the desires fueling an organization are fitting and God sized.

Founding leaders seem to have inexhaustible passion and energy for the cause driving the formation of the organization. Later generations often seem to have lost the vision, drive and passion. This decline of the heart may often precede the decline of the structure of the organization. Could this be why God is continually birthing new organizational expressions as others decay and die? Scripture and history tell repeated stories of God's people raising up new ministry expressions out of the death of other structures. Could we advance the work of Christ by holding some organizational funerals and being more open to new births?

Bottom Line: God may be the one ending the life cycle of an organization. If that is the case should it be viewed as his merciful hand creating space for new life to be expressed and a fresh work of God to be performed?

THINKING IT THROUGH:

1. In your organization, can you see drift from the original purpose of its creation?
2. Have perspectives on the following aspects of organizational culture affected the health of the organization where God has placed you?
   - Plans and view of the future
   - Value on people over structure
   - Organizational values shifting from empowering people for service to consuming and being served by the people
   - Shrinking of the vision of many of the people is paralyzing significant change

Chapter 4

The Symptoms of a Declining, Unhealthy Organization

What triggers an organization to shift from an incline/growth stage to a plateau and then decline stage? A single, often unstated value is given permission to take root and pushes the organization over the top and into decline. This often unstated and usually hidden value is, "Our major job is to preserve and protect the past".

The leaders are acutely aware of the challenges and cost people have incurred to raise the organization to a point of stable existence. It is attractive to now shift the focus of leadership to avoiding challenges. New ideas are measured against how they will shake up the current structure, not their potential in movement toward organizational purposes.

Many declining organizations living to preserve and protect spend a great deal of leadership energy in perfecting the systems. Bylaws, policy manuals, and detailed plans outlining how the members can conduct the coming year in much the same manner as the previous year become a barrier to change. While many of these elements can be helpful, they often become anchors to keep the organization in place.

For example, a procedure manual is a good tool enabling leaders to conserve energy as they process decisions without treating every one as a precedent. It also serves as a template to reflect and distill what has been gained in previous experience. But if the unstated agenda for these organizational refinements becomes a tool to resist change these tools lead against the flow of creativity and risk which is vital to a living walk of faith. In declining organizations the refined structure becomes a source of security and safety displacing God as the refuge.

DECLINING ORGANIZATIONS EXPERIENCE AN UNEVEN RATE OF DECAY

Aging in the biological life cycle often becomes a series of small losses punctuated by a major loss which then triggers other major losses.

Example
A person's weight creeps up, just a few more pounds each year, and in turn slowly decreases the energy level. The additional weight may also "shift" into certain parts of the body decreasing flexibility and range of motion. Vision and hearing may erode so slowly that the person fails to even notice the loss. Then one day a poorly placed step on the stairs results in a fall and a hip, which has become brittle in small increments over several years, shatters. Now, in a moment of crisis, a series of major decisions have to be made. The home place is closed and the person is moved into long-term care. Driving the car and a large degree of independence are lost forever.

The uneven rate of decline may follow a similar trajectory for an organization. The reality of decline is easy to deny until it is almost too late to correct and lengthen the healthy productive years of the organization.

DECLINING ORGANIZATIONS USUALLY REQUIRE A CRISIS BEFORE THEY WILL FACE REALITY

Many of the reclining or seriously declining organizations who contact me for consulting feel that a painful failure has forced them to consider reaching out for help. They want escape or relief from the circumstances that threaten the life of the organization.

Examples of a crisis that triggers a call for help could be:
- Failing to receive the income for the general budget
- A major push for funds for a new facility crashes and does not produce enough resources to even begin to act on the plan
- Key leaders resign their positions and/or volunteer leaders leave or move to the sidelines to observe and see what will happen next. I have placed a shaded circle in the life cycle diagram to indicate this critical moment.

> *In declining organizations the refined structure becomes a source of security and safety displacing God as the refuge.*

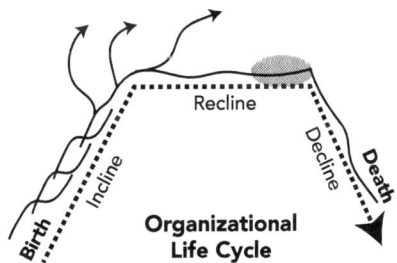

Example

In the life of an individual this crisis could be when they experience the "first heart incident". Picture a male, in his early fifties, 30 pounds overweight, no vacation in three years, long hours under stressful work, junk food, and couch potato lifestyle—and now a wakeup call—the first heart "incident".

What do the doctors ask the man?
- "Do you want to live for a short time or a longer time?"
- "What do you want the quality of the life you have left to be?"
- "Do you want to push yourself into major surgery?"

Bottom line: the doctors are attempting to get his attention.

The good news in this crisis involves a strong motivation to practice basic habits of a healthy life (proper diet, rest and exercise). This way of life should have been part of the adult lifestyle since the early twenties, but must now be intentionally implemented as disciplines that transform how the person lives. The doctor's prescription calls the patient to serious, radical repentance. Many habits must be abandoned *right now* and many new habits formed or reformed. The reality is that most patients know deep inside that they have ignored the guidelines of a healthy lifestyle. They have been living in self-deception, believing that the rules did not apply to them.

There are also basic lifestyle habits of walking with God. The steps of engagement, evangelism, and discipleship which contribute to developing a healthy spiritual heart, maturing in faith, hope and love are God's design for every Jesus follower. Somewhere along the way these very basic disciplines became fondly told memories of the past but have been lost to the present experience. Christians talk about the messy early years like a couple recalling the first few years of financial struggle in their marriage.

But all of those risky adventures are in the past. They have lost the desire to be in a place where the resources are few, and the creativity and risk are high. They have attempted to create a lifestyle that allows them to avoid the almost helpless sense of dependence on God and replace it with "blessings" of comfortable, clean predictability of a "church potato" lifestyle.

DOES ORGANIZATIONAL LIFE FOLLOW A SIMILAR PATTERN?

It is amazing that some who have the first heart attack fail to make the simple prescribed lifestyle changes. They may make some attempts, and the first few months bring hope from the new steps being taken, but somehow the changes do not really "take". Like a wave breaking on the beach, the crisis subsides and life drifts back into the tidal pools of unhealthy habits.

Leaders in declining organizations hasten the decline if they are afraid to call for the deep level of surrender and repentance needed. They may fear that the level of conflict will be too great because of the degree of change needed and then take the path of least resistance, backing down. The organization fails to learn the lessons from the "heart incident". Some will blame a pastor or other staff member and think the cure is simply in swapping leaders. Others will turn on fellow leaders. Blame and denial become ways to direct energy away from intentional repentance and needed changes.

Leaders may also seek to avoid the cost of long term endurance and go on a quest for a "magic pill" which will suddenly (ideally in no more than three months to a year) bring the organization back into vital health. In most cases the organization did not get into unhealthy recline and decline in a a short period of time and there are no magic pills that can quickly reverse the process. It is not unusual to see the senior leader being jettisoned, with the assumption that the solution will come through a new body in the top leadership chair. This new leader may bring valuable contributions to an organization, but remember there is only one Savior.

> There are no substitutes for daily steps of faith.

There are no substitutes for daily steps of faith. These faith steps are the risky, but exciting, journey of holding God's hand. These steps are made with a God-focused hope that endures like a long distance runner putting one foot in front of another mile after mile, and love joyfully sacrificing for the beloved.

But in declining organizations a spirit of fear often chokes out steps of faith. Addiction to fads, jumping to the next shortcut, and attempting to copy what God is doing somewhere else displaces enduring, steadfast, creative, positive hope. A consuming, "What is in it for me?" lust blocks the vessels of a heart designed by its creator for a flow of sacrificial, laying-down-life kind of love.

UNHEALTHY ORGANIZATIONS ARE FUELED BY FEAR

Fear has many masks. Leaders often use bureaucracy and paperwork as a low risk substitute for sitting down in honest conversation. Where fear dictates the choices of leaders, the result will be expressions of denial, pride, and selfishness. There will many hours spent in "us" and "them" and "win/lose" types of conversations.

Declining organizations cultivate a culture of control to minimize or avoid risk. One indicator of whether an organization is being fueled by faith or fear is to examine how "conversation" takes place. When people use e-mail or letters to confront instead of a face to face encounter they are usually avoiding relational risk in other ways as well.

The fear culture reeks with the smell of death and rotting carnal flesh. Around a dying person lights are kept low, conversations are held at low volume off in the shadows, and frequently no one wants to talk openly with the person about what is really going on. Truth becomes a rare commodity. When fear drives leaders they only say, at least in public, what they sense people want to hear. People talk to everyone about the problems except those who could do something about the concern. Gossip, disunity, and selfishness thrive in the declining organization.

Small issues that really don't matter become major topics of debate. In Jesus' day it was issues like hand washing, Sabbath practices and avoiding contact with certain people that allowed the religious leaders to avoid their heart and the major work God wanted to do in them.

Since it is only faith that pleases God, the fear-dominated organizational culture must be confronted, repented of, and replaced with a culture of trust, endurance and devotion.[12] A new draft of a 10-year plan or a fresh vision statement with updated graphics will not help what is lacking in relational integrity. What is needed is a room full of hearts open to each other and God in desperate hunger to see him act and be glorified in and through them. The people in the organization must be called to join Jesus in the garden and pray a prayer of surrender to God's will.

DECLINING ORGANIZATIONS LIVE FOR THE SHORT TERM

Strategies to pursue comfort, ease, stability, and to avoid pain fill up the calendar. In contrast, Jesus spoke often of investing the present moment for long-term heavenly reward.[13] Unhealthy Christian organizations often define the blessing of God as the absence of pain or risk. This is in sharp contrast to the vision of God's blessing to his people so they in turn become a blessing to others. He pours blessing *through* his people. In a declining organization, personal comfort becomes the new definition of blessing and the focus of prayers.

> Unhealthy Christian organizations define the blessing of God as the absence of pain or risk.

DECLINING ORGANIZATIONS ARE OFTEN VERY BUSY PLACES

Many declining organizations are choking on high levels of activity.

They are drowning in a full service menu providing a buffet of blessing for those who are members of the organization. Remember the parable of the seed being choked out by the thorns. Go back to Jesus' commentary on the parable and make a list of what the weeds really represent.[14]

Healthy organizations give resources away. Effective and vibrant groups invest the resources God has provided in people who need God. Unhealthy organizations fill the garage, basement and attics with stuff they are determined to hold on to with a death grip. This selfish abundance creates confusion and adds complexity to the organization. Every decision up for discussion ends up being weighed down by so many competing factors that it becomes almost impossible to move forward. New people are lost in a maze that only long-timers can navigate. This "hoarding" cancels the influence of the organization on anyone who does not know all of the written and unwritten rules.

Many people never make it to the mission field because they settle down and fill up their lives with cars, home, and other obligations, which may not be wrong in themselves, but are dead weight for a person on the move. Many churches need a good fire or at least a clean sweep garage sale to free the leadership to introduce changes that engage the people in "tearing down the gates of hell" advances.

THINKING IT THROUGH:

1. Read this passage and note any application to your life or leadership:
   May the God of peace, who through the blood of the eternal covenant brought back from the dead our Lord Jesus, that great Shepherd of the sheep, equip you with everything good for doing his will, and may he work in us what is pleasing to him, through Jesus Christ, to whom be glory for ever and ever. Amen.
   —Hebrews 13:20-21

2. Look back over the list of characteristics of reclining and declining organizations. Are any of these present in your organization? How can you pray about them?

Chapter 5

Practices of Vibrant & Effective Organizations

Have you ever heard any of comedian Jeff Foxworthy's "redneck jokes"? They all follow the same pattern. "You might be a redneck if... your house has wheels and your car sits in the yard on blocks."

Well, your organization might be inclining if... you are practicing vigorous continual assessment.

Effective organizations measure everything. If the organizations leaders are investing time or money on an activity in pursuit of their purposes, it is continually evaluated.

WHAT DOES BIBLICALLY BASED EVALUATION LOOK LIKE?

Let's revisit an outline of the biblical purposes of the church. They have been outlined in different ways by leaders seeking to focus disciples strategically.

Gene Getz, over 40 years ago, wrote of two purposes: edification and evangelism.[15] Chuck Swindoll used the acrostic W.I.F.E. (the church as the bride of Christ) to help churches focus on the purposes of worship, instruction, fellowship and evangelism.[16] Rick Warren introduced a baseball diamond visual for the five purposes of worship, loving, growing, serving, and sharing.[17]

One thing these various lists have in common is that they seek to describe a healthy gathering of Christians in terms of "being" and "doing". The New Testament lays out clear commands and principles for what Jesus followers are to *be* and what they should be *doing* together.

A clear and balanced description of the purpose of the church is found in Unit Two of Robertson McQuilkin's *The Five Smooth Stones: Essential Principles for Biblical Ministry*. The illustration below encapsulates the primary components of this purpose.

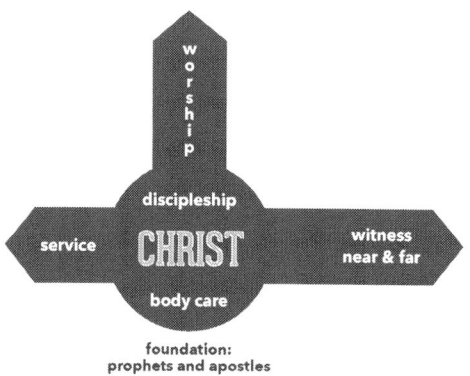

For each critical function leadership asks questions to determine if the money, time and gifting of God's people is carrying out these purposes.

Leadership continually revisits the "right questions". Below are some statements of a purpose centered church based on Robertson's work. **As you read each statement, think about a question to use in evaluating church under the functional authority of the Bible.**[18]

A purpose centered church is one where...
1. Worship is defined biblically in terms of whole-life worship. The music ministry is God focused, not man-focused, and developed in a way that all can fully participate emotionally and spiritually.
2. The teaching ministry of the church is multi-faceted, including small group accountability, and the results in spiritual transformation and growth are evident.
3. Member care reaches beyond spiritual pastoring to full-service emotional, physical, and material responsibility for all members.

4. The congregation has programs and involvement in mercy ministries to the community at home and abroad.
5. It is assumed that every member has a Spirit given ability (gift) to minister. The church has a program and leadership in place to help every member discover, develop to the full, and deploy his or her gifting and calling.
6. People understand that talents, while not the same as Spirit given gifts, but given in creation and growth, should be invested for Gods' glory.
7. When some purpose of the church is less than optimally fulfilled, the leaders and members "desire earnestly" in prayer for the Spirit to provide the gifts necessary.
8. Corporate prayer is pervasive (involving a majority of members, and in many formats), vital, expectant (faith-filled), and focused on spiritual needs of the congregation, the community and the unreached of the world, not just on the physical needs of the members.
9. The constantly articulated goal is for all members to be faithful witnesses in life and speech.
10. Teaching and training are provided to guide and empower for effective witness. Evidence is seen in consistent "body-life reproduction."
11. Leaders are constantly on the look-out for those who might be evangelistically gifted and provide training and encouragement to make them ever more effective.
12. The church body is knowledgeable and concerned about the unreached of the world, and a steady stream of career missionaries moves out from the congregation.
13. Short-term ministry and financial provision for God's people

away from home are carefully planned and harnessed to maximize Kingdom effectiveness.
14. Prayer for global outreach is informed, vital, and pervasive throughout the body, throughout the year.
15. Great effort is put into in helping people progress in their level of investment in God's activity around them.

Evaluation is not always a written inventory. It should also be part of the culture to be asking how everything is going and how it can be improved. Leaders should be in ongoing evaluation conversations. For example, here are four questions used in a weekly pastoral staff meeting to help the staff members focus their time on the right purposes.

1. How did you invest time with pre-Christians this past month?
2. How did you invest time developing new Christians?
3. How did you invest time in developing leaders?
4. How did you invest time in self-leadership development of your private, personal and public spheres of influence?

By the way, the pastoral staff members are not penalized for admitting struggles in these four questions. But, they are coached and held accountable to see improvement. For people to grow from facing hard questions there must be a "safe place" where grace and truth are mixed in equal portions to empower change and growth.

Rigorous intentional evaluation and assessment in some Christian organizations is viewed as unspiritual—it is argued that this is seeking to measure outcomes only God can give. We should carefully examine our questions, yardsticks, and benchmarks to ensure that they align with the questions God asks his people. Spiritual blindness and deafness was a major problem among the Jews of the first century. They saw and heard truth but were unwilling to use their eyes to see or their ears to hear how it connected to their hearts. John Gardner of Common Cause says, "Most ailing organizations have developed a functional blindness to their own defects. They are not suffering because they cannot solve their problems, but because they cannot see their problems."[19]

Healthy evaluation that challenges us to examine our actions closely helps to make sure that we are "seeing" and "hearing" the connection between what we know and are doing. Good evaluation helps us pull weeds that choke out fruitful work. Helpful assessment is a normal activity of any good steward/manager. A heart that is not seeing and hearing clearly is a divided heart.

Teach me your way, O LORD, and I will walk in your truth; give me an undivided heart, that I may fear your name. I will praise you, O Lord my God, with all my heart; I will glorify your name forever. — Psalm 86:11-12

Amaziah was twenty five years old when he became king, and he reigned in Jerusalem twenty-nine years. His mother's name was Jehoaddin; she was from Jerusalem. He did what was right in the eyes of the LORD, but not wholeheartedly. — 2 Chronicles 25:1-2

YOUR ORGANIZATION MIGHT BE INCLINING IF...
YOUR LEADERS HAVE A MATURE PERSPECTIVE ON CONFLICT

Healthy leaders understand that when people show up filled with questions, even if the questions are delivered with some anger, they need to receive them.

If there is an attacking manner in the approach of the person it provides a character development teaching moment. In a painful confrontation it will help the leader to respond properly by giving thanks that somebody feels strongly about something. One of my mentors, Ron Barker, has often said, "It is easier to tame the demoniac than to raise the dead!" Strong emotion may not always be justified but it does indicate passion and perhaps even a deep desire for the organization to be effective.

YOUR ORGANIZATION MIGHT BE INCLINING IF... LEADERS ARE OPEN TO QUESTIONS

Revisiting good questions is a means of keeping us before God in a place of healthy humility. God delights in the pliable heart of soft potter's clay. When leaders are teachable and anticipating his correction, guidance and grace in their walking with him, he delights to walk with us.

"He lets the proud walk alone as they desire, but he walks closely with the humble" (Roy's paraphrase).

Leaders who chop off the heads of those raising the tough questions, or who only surround themselves with people who agree with them, are in a dangerous place. An unwillingness to be exposed by a probing question usually indicates pride and a desire to cover up what deep down we fear may be wrong.

Recall that the life cycle divides organizational life into three stages: incline, recline and decline. The incline stage could be broken down further into "birth", "childhood", "adolescence", and "early adulthood." What constitutes the right questions for an organization to ask changes with every stage.

The birth stage

In "birth" there is a blank page and the leaders are simply asking how to invest the few resources they have to make maximum impact.

- What is critical to our survival and should have most of our focus?

- How do we get new people in?
- How do we get everyone contributing their time and energy?
- How do we get people to support this cause?
- Who is praying?
- Are our families surviving our sacrificial investment of time?

The childhood stage

As the fragile newborn moves into childhood the challenges become one of taking the many "firsts". The first step, first word, first tying of shoes by a young child parallel organizational "firsts" such as, the first mission partnership, the first multiplication of small groups, and the first church discipline crisis.

- Who has the camera? Did you get a picture/video of *that*?
- We have never done… (Fill in blank with almost everything) before. How do we do it?
- Will we perform basic practices like singing, baptism, communion, collecting offerings based on the experiences we have had in our past, or does this need to be different to capture and express the biblical values we are seeking to live out?
- A church helping to sponsor us has offered --- a communion set of plates and trays, OR their previous year's Vacation Bible School curriculum, OR an invitation to participate in an evangelism rally. Do we receive the gift and hide it in the closet until the next yard sale? Do we just go with it? Do we carefully decline?
- A friend is going into missions and has asked for our support. Do we ignore his e-mail and hope we don't run into each other? Do we seek to get the leadership to see this as a faith exercise and go for it? Do we take the time right now to work on how our vision and values will be lived out in our missions giving?

The adolescence stage

As the organization matures there is a wildness that comes with discovering new levels of teenage like energy and resource. There is a flood of good ideas and the "good" questions are ones that help the leaders determine priorities and separate the good from the best.

- Why can't we do every good idea someone has read about, heard on Christian radio, or was done in their previous church?
- We want everyone to be involved, but how do we also tell them leadership dissolves if everyone is doing their own thing?
- Everyone has an opinion but who is willing to commit to really sacrifice and follow through?
- Do we continue to handle every decision or do we form some policies that express our values and speed up decisions on some things?
- One great question, I picked up hearing Andy Stanley speak on conflict, "Is this a tension to manage or a problem to solve?" Once I started using this question I realized how much energy I was investing poorly seeking to solve a problem when it was really going to be an ongoing tension we would need to manage. I like to solve problems because we can then file them away and leave a clean spot on our desk. Tensions never leave the desk. As we manage them there may be times when they move to the back of the desk, but they are never finished. This question often applies in many of the life stages but it is certainly a valuable companion in the wild messy teen years of the organization.

The early adulthood stage

In early adulthood we choose long-term relationships and often begin to have our own children. There is a need to plan for the future, and determine what percentage of resources will be "saved" for future opportunities instead of pouring them all out on the present situations.

- At what level can we partner with organizations that differ from us on some beliefs or values?
- What aspects of the work do we invest paid staff energy in and which do we seek to continue with volunteers?
- Where are the leaders? How do we discover and develop and deploy enough leaders for all of the opportunities around us?
- What facilities do we need to serve the organization?

YOUR ORGANIZATION MIGHT BE INCLINING IF...
THERE IS FREQUENT ORGANIZATIONAL REPENTANCE

I am using repentance to seek a fresh word for describing radical organizational decision-making. *Personal* repentance is "turning from" and "turning to".[20] *Organizational* repentance is stopping and making needed realignment. Continual refocusing corrects the natural tendency to turn inward or turn away from walking with God in his purposes. Organizational life has many parallels to organic life. Plants will grow out in many directions and require a gardener willing to intentionally cut if the plant is to be effectively fruitful.

Pruning creates capacity

Just look at apple trees that have been carefully pruned each year and then contrast it to the quantity and quality of the fruit from an old tree that has gone many years without pruning.

Too often when I come in as a consultant I feel like I have entered an archeological dig with all of the layers of years of life exposed.

Example

Sunday school was evaluated and instead of making needed changes the leaders added another layer of Sunday evening small groups.

A few years later, as a result of evaluation, it was determined that most of the small groups were weak in making disciples. The church leaders did not want to threaten or stir up the small group leaders and members loyal to the program so they discussed the problems but took no action. Out of fear, and to do something new in an area of church life where they would get little resistance, the leaders launched a high profile church wide men's and women's ministry.

You get the idea where this story is going, right?

Twenty years down the road there are layers upon layers of mediocre ministries which are only marginally effective in accomplishing biblical purposes. There is no margin to add anything new or any breathing leaders which would be needed to add a new layer.

The decisions made out of fear led to many layers. These layers often feed the competition among programs with each making a case for a share of resources even though they are actually supposed to be working together toward the same purpose. This layering also limits the personal growth of those leading and faithfully seeking to make the programs in each layer work. At some point it begins to cave in on itself. The good thing is there so many layers and people involved at overlapping purposes that there are lots of people to blame (satirical humor inserted here)!

There are three ways for leaders to choose to invest the life of an individual or organization:

1. Do nothing
2. Do too many things—the distracted, busy, shallow life
3. Do a few things— those placed in your path by God (Matt. 25:21)

This is how we know [ASSESSMENT] *that we love the children of God: by loving God and carrying out his commands. This is love for God:* [ACTION ALIGNMENT] *to obey his commands. And his commands are not burdensome.* —1 John 5:2-3

Everyone who competes in the games goes into [ALIGNMENT] *strict training. They do it to get a crown that will not last; but we do it to get a crown that will last forever. Therefore I do not run like a man* [ASSESSMENT] *running aimlessly; I do not fight like a man beating the air.* —1 Corinthians 9:25-26

YOUR ORGANIZATION MIGHT BE INCLINING IF...
YOU EMBRACE LIVING IN A MESSY ORGANIZATIONAL LIFE

Notice that in my simple visual of the life cycle the "incline" side of the cycle is not one smooth upward swing but many spurts, births, restarts, and new expressions. Instead of finding something that works and then staying with it until it dies, leaders carefully observe how the context around them is changing. In addition they pay attention to how the people in the organization are changing (new people arrive, others leave, as well as many people growing). They anticipate and actually give permission for experiments, creative risks, and new ventures which will flow in alignment with the mission.

At times, the leaders will detect there has been mission drift and they will kill or dismantle some structures that many casual observers would say are working fine. They have a learning spirit that says we must go back to the foundation, assume we know nothing, and rebirth. Willow Creek Church leaders say that at any given time 20% of their ministry structures are in forced "remodeling" from the ground up. It gives the organization the feel of always being under construction, and never being finished. It is intentional flexibility. All tactical ministry efforts are viewed as experiments and rough drafts which are porous to absorbing changes and adjustment as needed.

In the biblical account Daniel and his three friends became change agents to the training structure imposed on them. How? In a chapel message at Columbia International University[21] Junias Venugopal pointed out that these young leaders in training functioned as thermostats not thermometers. A thermometer only reflects and records the temperature while a thermostat brings the room temperature into alignment with its standard. Leaders in healthy organizations are thermostats.

YOUR ORGANIZATION MIGHT BE INCLINING IF...
ENERGY IS BEING INVESTED TO MAKE SURE PEOPLE KNOW THEY MATTER

In effective organizations people are treasured the way God treasures them. The leaders are committed to never leaving one of their own behind on the battlefield. These leaders possess a shepherd's heart going looking for the one lost from the ninety-nine. They do not shoot those wounded for their sinful choices.

They cultivate a culture where there is a freedom to fail. I am not primarily speaking of sinful failure but of simply missing a goal or trying something that does not produce the anticipated result. Wounding (sinful actions) and failures (faithful service with a learning opportunity) both require wise application of grace and truth. In healthy organizations there are costly investments of relational energy yielding fruits of healing, restoration, learning, and growth.

YOUR ORGANIZATION MIGHT BE INCLINING IF...
THERE ARE SEASONS OF GRIEVING THE LOSS OF PEOPLE

While leaders are committed deeply to an environment that reflects God's heart for people, they are not forcing or manipulating people into staying in the organization. Jesus never begged, forced or manipulated followers. People may choose, for a variety of reasons, to not stay with the organization as it moves along in its journey.

Sometimes those who leave may gain perspective through the distance and return. They have experienced a personal surgery with God setting them free from fears or resistance of the changes. Some people may simply need another environment to live out their walk with God. And some may be like the people who simply turned and followed Jesus no more.

People breaking away, or those who are moved along by God assigning them to another expression of service are some of the relational painful losses leaders grieve. Learning to mourn is essential for those who will endure in leadership.[22]

YOUR ORGANIZATION MIGHT BE INCLINING IF...
PEOPLE ARE ENJOYING AND ENCOURAGING BOTH DIRECT AND FACILITATIVE MINISTRY

Leaders enjoy contributing their gifts to the work of God in human hearts. But an even greater joy is seeing people around them beginning to contribute what God has entrusted to them. Leading requires being "player/coaches". The leaders may run, block or tackle, but the effective player/coaches know the most strategic part of their work is when they are assisting others on the team in being effective.

Does it often take more time to do something "through" or "with" someone else for the sake of their development versus doing it myself? Yes! But as we can observe in both God's creation and redemptive dramas he does not place the priority on efficiency that some cultures do. God is surely effective but often extravagant, patient, and goes to the extreme to connect with and involve us in his work. I often use the quote, "Most of my fruit grows on other trees" to remind me of the value in facilitating the ministry of others.

YOUR ORGANIZATION MIGHT BE INCLINING IF... OPEN HEART SURGERY HAS BECOME A NORMAL OCCURRENCE AND IS NOT REALLY A "BIG THING"

Open heart surgery is taking place when people feel safe they can risk being vulnerable and express an authentic need for God's touch. They know God's surgical tools are often other people in the spiritual family. This level of deep personal change is not like a cosmetic makeover simply covering flaws.

Instead, we acknowledge the depth of our motives and expectations that color everything we see and what we reveal to others. We all live with three spheres of influence and responsibility around us. The outer circle is our public world. People touching our public life usually only see what we plan for them to see. We control what is known about us. Our inner circle is our personal world. Family, friends, and close associates see us in more unguarded moments. They observe more of our life so they know more of who we really are, and what our heart values. But even in our personal world we hide and determine levels of disclosure. In our private world only we, as individuals, and God are the audience. We may choose to let part of our private world show into our personal or public worlds, but we can also close out aspects of it—even to our spouse.

When God works in the human heart he touches all of these circles. But he is never content to only work in the public or even personal world. He is always aiming at the private, the heart, the intimate place where he lives and connects with the real us. Leaders in effective and vibrant organizations understand God's target for heart level change and actively and actively participate in the process.

YOUR ORGANIZATION MIGHT BE INCLINING IF... THERE ARE CELEBRATIONS

How can we read passages like 1 Corinthians 15 or 2 Corinthians 5 and not see that God is all about resurrection, restoring glory and new creation? God's physical world, even in its groaning with sin and death, still reflects his love for change. Change is very similar to physical movement. Change is an expenditure of energy influencing movement. Movement in the organic world is one indication of life. It is the same with our created structures. Change is an indicator of life. No change? Check the pulse! Reread Luke 15. One common experience in all 3 parables of the lost being found is a party! It grieves me to see us celebrate the completion of a building, or the anniversary of the organization's birth, but invest so little in celebrating the aspects of kingdom life God leads heaven in celebrating.

YOUR ORGANIZATION MIGHT BE INCLINING IF...
PEOPLE ARE NOT SURPRISED THAT CHANGE (MOVEMENT) HAS CREATED A LEVEL OF CONFLICT (HEAT)

Lay down this book or e-reader for a moment. Place your palms together and begin to move them back and forth against each other. Your hands were created to "fit" and yet these incredibly similar body parts create friction in their movement.

Christian leaders should be those who celebrate change just like the angels in heaven rejoice over the "change" of one sinner's heart. At the same time, leaders are in tune with the reality of sin's pollution of the human heart and the basic resistance to God's will that is present throughout creation. Leaders in inclining organizations are not surprised by conflict. They expect conflict to be present and approach it with both

> Most things wrong in an individual's or organization's life are the result of failing to do the right things.

God's truth (the fuel for change through asking questions, learning, and experimenting) and God's grace (the oil of authenticity, vulnerability, healing compassionate care, and a thankful praise filled spirit).

Most things wrong in an individual's or organization's life are the result of failing to do the right things. Many of our changes are really steps of repenting; turning so we can go in the right direction. Repentance is *the* path of transformation with God. As we come under his touch he is making us more like Christ. His touch will always include a loving assault on our pride and a submission of humbly accepting his will being best.[23] Needed organizational change is often simply one part of God's way to get at individual repentance and our relational conflicts are the heat needed to thaw the unresponsive heart.

In marriage one says "no" to all other possible spouses in order to say "yes" to the beloved. During the wedding the man and woman are not even aware of the "no" they are declaring to all other potential partners because his or her heart is responding to the loved one with a declaration of "yes, yes, yes". God is working into the hearts of his disciples that same kind of loving, relaxed, unforced obedience to his will.

There is a glorious, messy, uncomfortable, rewarding, exhilarating and sacrificial life for leaders in the inclining stages of organizational life. It is worth it. I have been praying during the time of writing this book that will God will allow me a few more assignments in the leadership of effective and vibrant organizations. There will come a stage in my life to just be a human being and much less a human doer…. But I am not ready to be put out to pasture just yet!

THINKING IT THROUGH:

1. Read these passages on the heart and apply them to leading an inclining/growing life and organization.

I run in the path of your commands, for you have set my heart free. — Psalm 119:32

Whom have I in heaven but you? And earth has nothing I desire besides you. — Psalm 73:25

I said to the LORD, "You are my Lord; apart from you I have no good thing." — Psalm 16:2

What is more, I consider everything a loss compared to the surpassing greatness of knowing Christ Jesus my Lord, for whose sake I have lost all things. I consider them rubbish, that I may gain Christ and be found in him, not having a righteousness of my own that comes from the law, but that which is through faith in Christ—the righteousness that comes from God and is by faith. I want to know Christ and the power of his resurrection and the fellowship of sharing in his sufferings, becoming like him in his death, and so, somehow, to attain to the resurrection from the dead. — Philippians 3:8-11

2. Review the characteristics of inclining organizations. Select the ones that need to be reviewed often to maintain a correct perspective.
3. Are there characteristics that you need to discuss with the leaders in the organization?
4. Are there ministries that need pruning? What would pruning to increase capacity look like?
5. Instead of adding new layers, what would it look like to use the current situation as a teachable moment to develop those involved in this ministry?

6. According to the life stage of the organization where you serve, create some good questions you need to be asking often that will keep you in alignment with walking out a faith adventure of redemptive love.

Chapter 6

The Importance of Seeing the Seasons of a Work Cycle

God has created this world so that most of what is produced develops over a cycle of seasons from seed to fruit. This biological progression was a common experience of Adam's original work as he tended the garden.[24] After the rebellion by Adam and Eve to their creator's rule, God increased the resistance that would accompany Adam's work. God did not remove our desire for productive work but he did insert hurdles to fruitfulness: "in pain you shall eat of it all of the days of your life".[25]

God also broadened creation's resistance to our efforts at fruitfulness to include the woman's pain in the labor of bearing the fruit of a child. The seasons of conception, pregnancy, labor and delivery share many similar elements to the thorns among the seed bearing its fruit.

The seasonal cycle of fruitfulness in brief is:

1. Sowing
2. Nurturing
3. Protecting
4. Harvesting

SOWING – The farmer breaks up the soil so the seed can be easily buried. In a mysterious way, there in the damp darkness, God has placed life in the seed that breaks out and grows.[26]

NURTURING – God must provide the right amount of sun, rain and food for the growing plant to survive. The farmer can often contribute some supplemental water or fertilizer but in most cases the survival of the plants depends on God giving the essential contribution.

PROTECTING – There is opposition to growth. Bugs attack. Birds, rabbits and other animals make a meal out of the tender plant. Blight and disease can kill or damage the plant. Weeds threaten to choke it out. The good farmer invests the sweat to fight them all.

HARVESTING – Now comes the fruit. Often months of labor go by with very little fruit. Buds turn into blooms which then grow into the fruit which then slowly ripens. And at just the right moment, in a flurry of depleting around the clock investment of energy, the harvest is gathered before it spoils in the field.

These same four seasons are present in the work activities of a business, a church or ministry or almost any productive work we attempt. They may not be quite as sequential as the biological journey from seed to fruit but discerning the season gives good clues of the type of work required at the present moment.

Organizations not only go through stages that move them from birth to death, but they also go through seasons of fruit producing. A seasonal cycle is repeated many times in the life of the organization as it moves from stage to stage.

Picture your organization as a farm. If you could take photos over the life of the farm in one photo you would see a new barn being built and a shiny new tractor parked inside. Years later another photo shows the same barn now with a slight lean and the tractor is rusting. Those pictures depict the overall life cycle and its aging change over time.

The seasonal cycle is taking place in the garden, a larger field, and the chicken coop. The farmer, seeking to engage in fruitful work, may be plowing one area to receive the spring seed and the next day cutting a winter cover crop that is at harvest stage in another field, and putting medicine in the food for the chickens to protect them from an infection.

This parallels organizational life. The overall life stage will shape how one approaches the seasonal work that is needed. But in any organization of more than just a few people, there will be different seasons of work cycles going on at the same time.

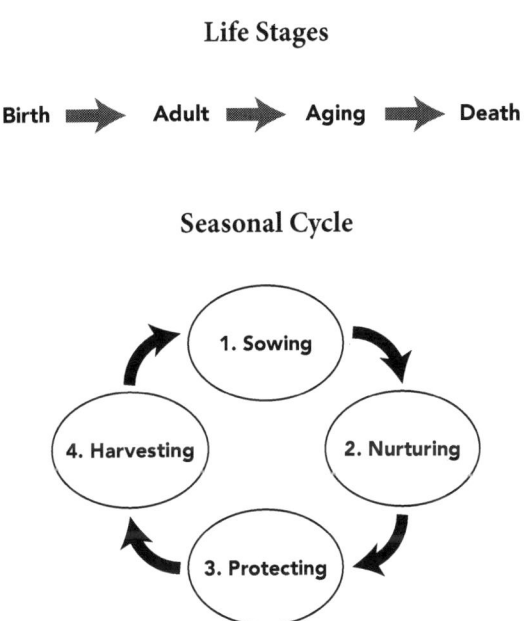

Example

A church in the early adult stage wants to give birth to a new expression of ministry. At this stage they have staff and volunteer resources that can be brought to bear on a worthy new work. They want to reproduce new ministry that is bearing redemptive fruit.

After research of the community they discover families in their community with special needs children. It is not surprising the parents do not feel that church is a safe place for them or their child. People who do not know the child may judge them as poor parents. The church environment may not provide adequate safety concerns or address specific needs of the child. The parents may not want their child to be a hindrance to the spiritual instruction of the typically developing children that the children's classes are designed to serve. But these families also have pressing needs for support, encouragement and a spiritual perspective on the challenges they face daily.

The families are often networked with other families with special needs. By investing in ministry suited to the families with whom they have some contact the word will spread quickly through this community.

The church leaders recognize this as a people group in their community who have limited access to the gospel because of the barriers to being a part of many church communities. They know that the love and compassion of Christ followers can make a significant and life changing contribution. The Gospel is surely good news from God for all people!

So the church leadership begins the journey of asking God to take the seed of an idea and a recently surfaced need and bring kingdom fruit for his glory. They step out with some element of risk and uncertainty. It is a faith adventure because they have never tackled this kind of ministry.

SOWING – We cast many ideas around. We brainstorm broadly. We "blue sky" think and pray and trust that from many of our creative thoughts at least a few will take root and begin to grow a solution to a problem, an answer to a need, or a victory to a challenge in our work.

The Example continues: They go and meet with families of special needs children they do know. They listen carefully, read widely, and are slow to judge whether any specific idea is workable. They look for ways God may already be at work in giving people a passion in this area. They seek to determine if God has already brought someone into the church with some background in working with special needs children.

NURTURING – Most new work goes through a season of fragile establishment. We do our best to invest what has been entrusted to us but we know that if God doesn't supply passionate leaders, finances, or other resources that are beyond our capacity the startup may die out.

The Example continues: They start small with a shadow program of special trained volunteers who focus on meeting the needs of the three families they already know. There is constant evaluation and a specific prayer support team to undergird the work.

PROTECTING – There are corruptions that can grow from within and there are enemies that may attack from the outside. Work always takes place on battlefields, or other places that are resistant to bearing fruit. It is an odd truth that the world needs the seed-to-fruit cycle to survive and yet the threats are often so great that fruitfulness seems impossible. God getting anything done in the church with the likes of us sinful workers is a miracle.

The Example continues: One of the families leaves with hurt and tears one Sunday when they overhear some people wrongly ascribing the behavior of their autistic child to a lack of good biblical discipline. A pastoral staff member must go to the family and also lead in deciding how to best communicate to all of the parents in the children's ministry the unique challenges the new family is facing. It is a messy, time consuming challenge to turn this pain into a teachable moment for everyone without placing the special needs children and their families in an unwanted spotlight of attention and pity.

HARVESTING – Nothing beats the juicy reward of ripe fruit. There is nothing like the "light bulb" coming on in a student's understanding as a reward to the teacher patiently sowing and working with students. There is nothing like sharing in the joy of a new Christian freshly liberated from the burdens of needing forgiveness and guilt removed. Paul describes the joy in the work of ministry where one plants and another waters but God gives the growth.[27] Jesus reminds the disciples of the joy of the sower and the reaper in God's harvest of souls.[28]

The Example continues: A small group in the church begins to provide respite care so two of the couples raising special needs children and who have no family close by can have a date night or even go shopping without always being a caravan. Two volunteer young ladies in the youth ministry are so enjoying being shadow assistants they are considering a career in special education. And one of the children with Down's syndrome is teaching everyone in the children's ministry how to really worship with a free passionate spirit.

HOW DOES THE SEASONAL CYCLE OF PRODUCTIVE LABOR APPLY TO THE STAGES OF THE LIFE CYCLE?

Some stages of life are more conducive to fruit bearing than others. Just ask most couples in their late fifties if they want to have more children! But as we know God specializes in taking the barren and bringing forth new life. His grace and power shine bright when the dead comes to life.

As a coach I encourage leaders to believe God for the fruit of "making disciples" regardless of the stage in the life cycle. But discerning the stage does help leaders know how to pray and helps them wisely invest the resources God has supplied. Often obedience to invest in kingdom purposes while living in organizational decline will call leaders to a faith challenge. Faith ignites a longing to see God provide the resources not visible at the present time for fruit bearing to occur. It is great for a 24-year-old and a 74-year-old to both be involved in a church plant. But on some level it may require a greater faith challenge for the older adult. Why? They are facing the reality of shrinking energy and earning power and stepping up to this challenge stretches them in ways the younger person may not see.

WORK IS REALLY ABOUT BEING FRUITFUL

Work is rarely satisfying if we sense we are just moving paper around on our desk. Work has a goal, a destination, a harvest as the motivating vision and energizing hope. We may need to stop our work in order to clarify the goal, outcome or desired results. A lack of clarity paralyzes decision making and leaves workers feeling like they are wandering in an endless maze.

Fruitful work is actually known to extend life and enhance health. The most fulfilled people I know, who have gone through retirement from one career, are still engaged in very productive labor. Boredom and making life all about one's own pleasure is the opposite of the loving life patterned after the love of Jesus. It is the loving life that really knows the abundant life God designed for his children.

WORK WILL ALWAYS ENCOUNTER RESISTANCE

When we engage in productive labor we frequently face the reality that our resources will not be enough. Humility is an attitude that approaches life's challenges by acknowledging we need help and the help required must come from outside of our self. God needs to show up or little lasting impact will be accomplished.

Resistance reminds us that our efforts, without God's resources are never enough. The pain God introduces into his creation in Genesis 3 serves a very valuable purpose of driving us to God. Just ask students who are praying before a test if they need God's help. Just ask teachers who are walking in to the classroom full of students if they need wisdom. The confidence that we were designed to bear fruit is tempered with the awareness that we are not enough.

> Resistance reminds us that our efforts, without God's resources are never enough.

FRUITFULNESS IS A MYSTERY

One aspect of seeing the seed grow into a fruitful plant is understanding and participating in its development. But, as Paul says three times in one short paragraph, God gives the growth.[29] Prayer is so foundational and essential in all of our work. Many of the examples of prayer in the Bible encourage us to pray specifically (to ask God for what we need to the best degree we can discern it) but also pray submissively (in humility acknowledging our limited perspective) trusting in his good heart to supply what he knows is best.

When I consult with an organization, regardless of the stage of life, I begin with an assessment of and restoring the priority of the prayer life of the members and leaders of the organization. I will never forget being in the headquarters of a ministry and watching as the leaders went in one room for a working committee meeting while the workers and volunteers gathered for a meal, communion and prayer. The leaders were failing to see the statement they were making every week about the lack of value they were placing on prayer and the community. Why don't we have time to pray with one another, and not just pray about physical illness, deaths or personal crisis, but launching out from those heart aches to enter into what God's heart aches to see for this world?

Mystery also limits the weight we can place on our planning. Farmers, doctors and church planters conduct research seeking to understand the mystery of the seed, the new business or the church plant. The need for investigation highlights our inability to predict the perfect formula that will guarantee the intended results. Some leaders continue to seek the five or seven critical elements guaranteeing success. The formulas do not work. Many with the "key" elements still fail and some organizations ignoring all of the formulas demonstrate vibrancy and effectiveness.

WORK TAKES TIME

A good farmer is a patient farmer. Shortcuts, fads, and miracle cures abound to speed up and reduce the effort in losing weight, getting rich, growing a church or doing almost anything. They are of little value and in most cases these schemes are a distraction to the work that is really needed. Save your money—there is no $19.95 quick fix to accomplishing fruitful work. Productive labor requires sustained effort over time. Work is exerting the right kind of effort that fits the season of the journey from seed to fruit. There is no shortcut. Endurance is kept alive by staying focused on a clear objective. The farmer never loses sight of the harvest. The athlete has pictures of the big race on the training room wall. The solider knows the objective of the mission.

Often the clear objective helping in visualizing is based on past experience. The harvest of three years ago, the race in the last Olympics, the battle for the other city all help the farmer, athlete and solider press on when the reality of failure seems more of a possibility than any kind of reward.

As for that in the good soil, they are those who, hearing the word, hold it fast in an honest and good heart, and bear fruit with patience. —Luke 8:15, ESV

Notice the phrase, "with patience" used by Jesus in the parable of the soils. The word means a hope filled endurance. An endurance that is covered in anticipation just like a child waiting for Christmas morning. This kind of patience is what we see in the eyes of a ministry team as we work through the seasons of laboring for a harvest.

WORK DEMANDS DISCERNING WHAT KIND OF EFFORT IS NEEDED AT THE RIGHT TIME

A good farmer discerns the season and gives the right kind of investment at the right time. Pull up weeds at the wrong time and you damage the plant growing nearby. Water the fields at the wrong time and the plants rot. Harvest too early and the fruit never ripens. Prune at the wrong time and you may miss a whole cycle of harvest or even kill the plant. Sow at the wrong time and the plant may never break ground before it is killed in a harsh cold.

THINKING IT THROUGH

1. Can you identify two examples from your ministry right now of how the development of fruitful work is moving through seasons?

Work Activity / Event	Sowing	Nurturing	Protecting	Harvesting

2. List the critical actions to accomplish or prayers that need to be answered for the current season of work to be completed well.
3. Look at all of the ministries in your organization. What type of seasonal work (Sowing, Nurturing, Protecting and Harvesting) is needed for each? Write a specific next action including who will assist you and when you will get started. After writing a draft show it to no one but God. Take some long walks and talk it through in prayer and ask for the Spirit to whisper to you what needs to be changed in the list and where you need to begin. Take time to actively listen to what God is saying to you.

Conclusion – Suggestions on How to Lead

LEADING FROM ANY STAGE IN THE LIFE CYCLE

1. People are treasured by God and will live for eternity so value people over structures, systems and programs. You may sense a leader on the team needs to dial back on investing in leading in the organization to focus on family or self-leadership. Don't be tempted to avoid a conversation to check-in and giving them permission to renegotiate commitments. Don't silently just hope they can keep going so your leadership plate does not get anything else added on.

Be very quick to thank others for their contribution and give examples and specifics highlighting the value of their serving.

2. Prayer is the greatest asset provided by God to empower change. Ask him for wisdom and creativity to generate a united and intentional prayer covering aligned with a clear vision of God's values and purposes. In many settings the weekly gathering in the evening or early morning at one location may not work. It will take fresh approaches to truly generate a community of praying people united in one heart. Prioritize the time and money needed to build toward that aim.

3. Trust is the greatest gift any person can develop with a leader. Be worthy of it. Earn it. Give it to others who are faithful. Be very aware of your motives. Impure motives erode trust. Keep your word.

LEADING FROM THE INCLINE STAGES OF THE LIFE CYCLE

1. Very early in the life of the organization, begin to evaluate everything you invest time and money doing. Design and invite assessment of your personal leadership. Be a lifelong learner.

2. Once you evaluate, take action. Make changes, prune back, refocus, experiment, keep clear on a very simple list of the purposes of the organization. Don't ask, "Does this program, activity or idea fit with our purposes?" Go beyond "fit" and ask, "Is this the best way we know right now and with the resources God has provided for us to work toward living out this purpose?"

3. When developing tactical plans for the next ministry cycle never start with just one idea. Insist the group come up with at least 3 plans and then decide. Working mentally to generate 3 valid plans will often surface fresh thinking and perspective.

LEADING FROM THE DECLINE STAGES OF THE LIFE CYCLE

1. Model and teach on grieving losses. Honest but grace filled conversations are a must. It will be easier to grow some hope for a future if we are being honest about the present.

2. Do not over promise or oversell the changes you are proposing. Honestly to admit the cost of change and don't forget the cost is more than just money. Most changes addressing serious life robbing challenges will also generate some problems and questions. Go ahead and agree with those resisting the change the result will not be problem or question free. Change must be packaged with a clear plan for evaluating and assessing the change and then making the next wave of adjusting refinements.

3. People are what last. Don't become so focused on seeking to extend the life cycle of the organization that you don't make time for evangelism, discipleship and leadership training. With your best effort, if the organization dies on your watch or continues in decline and dies after you are on to your next assignment, your investment in growing people will continue to bear fruit. People help birth the next generation of organizations. People can relocate and make valuable contributions

to God's kingdom in other organizations. God may allow you to lead a person to Christ who will become a leader in an organization that does not even exist today. What an honor!

A Prayer for Leaders

Father, we need leaders with Christ-courage who are ready to hold a funeral before they pray for a resurrection.

We need leaders who lead the way in repentance.

We need leaders who know how to lead, not from above, or even from below, but leading from among the people.

We need leaders to step back in order to gain a wise perspective but are not "armchair quarterbacks" who feel it is their right to shout instructions from the stands.

Lord, it is unnerving to consider but it is true. Organizations become like their leaders. To a large degree organizations do what the leaders and people pray about. Please help us repent of praying too small and with fear instead of faith.

Great Reconciler, we know that in a sinful world there will always be relational breakdowns. But just as the major story of the Bible is you reconciling us to yourself through Christ's suffering and death, give us leaders willing to embrace a ministry of reconciliation and the loving sacrifice we know it will require.

By faith we declare that until the mission of God for the church of making disciples among all people is fulfilled and Christ returns no Christian is ever unemployed.

In hope we affirm that organizations will surely decay and die and new organizations will be birthed from the passion and gifts invested by leaders and the people.

In love we desire to work with our brothers and sisters through these various frail organizations to demonstrate the truth and grace found abundantly in Christ our Lord.

For His Glory – Amen.

Resources

Would you like to receive a free e-mail that links you to fresh ministry resources? Go to www.royking.org

I have been learning about Life Cycle theory for several years. Here are some readings that apply it to churches and parachurch structures:

Arnold L. Cook. *Historical Drift: Must My Church Die?* Camp Hill, PA: Christian Publications, 2000. Arnold is past president of the CMA Canada. As a denominational leader he writes to both congregational and parachurch leaders. He offers hope through a biblical model of repentance, revival and renewal to extend the effective life of declining organizations.

George Bullard. "Congregational Passages," an occasional publication of the National Consultant for Denominational Transformation, Vol. One, No. One, (August, 1996) George can be reached through www.bullardjournal.org. He has many self-published articles, reflections, and research on the life cycle applied to congregations. George is a national church consultant.

Terry Walling. *Refocusing Leaders* and *Refocusing Churches* are available from ChurchSmart Publications (800-253-4276). Terry has become a mentor and friend who has taken the leadership emergent theory concepts framed by Bobby Clinton and applied them to leaders and organizations. I am especially grateful to the CRM (Church Resource Ministries) team, including Gary Mayes, who instructed me on life cycle theory in their Refocusing training workshops.

Martin Robinson & Dwight Smith. *Invading Secular Space: Strategies for Tomorrow's Church.* London: Monarch Books, 2003. Martin is a church consultant in the UK. Dwight is president of Saturation Church Planting Intl and has taught as at Columbia Intl. University. Chapter six deals specifically with life cycle but this is a helpful book written in the format of consultants seeking to coach church leaders into multiplication strategies.

Hans Finzel. *Change is Like a Slinky: 30 Strategies for Promoting and Surviving Change in Your Organization.* Chicago: Northfield, 2004. Hans is the president of World Venture (formerly known as CBInternational) Chapter 22 deals with assessing your organization from a life cycle perspective and offers probing questions. Hans writes as one journaling a season of major change in an established mission agency.

Michael Frost & Alan Hirsch. *The Shape of Things to Come: Innovation and Mission for the 21st Century Church.* Peabody, MA: Hendrickson Publishers, 2003. Two Australian church leaders outline a global perspective on the church and practical strategies emerging in a the new global context. Starting on page 177 they connect the APEPT model (Apostle, Prophet, Evangelist, Pastor, Teacher) of cluster leaders to life cycle theory. They suggest which types of leadership contribution are most relevant to each life stage.

Notes

1. Robert Clinton is now retired. He directed my D.Min with a focus on Leadership at Fuller Theological Seminary. Dr. Clinton is an alumnus of Columbia International University and was also involved for several years with leadership training for World Team. His resources are available at http://bobbyclinton.com

2. Dr. Steve Sweatman is now the President of Missionary Training International.

3. David Olson, *The American Church in Crisis*. I watch these stats on a regular basis from several different sources. Be careful of using them for more than a range. Some only count denominational reports, and do not include groups like Calvary Chapel that do not have membership rolls. Also house churches, a growing edge of new works, are often not included.

4. I do not have stats on mission agencies or other non-profit organizations. Through coaching and consulting with some of them it seems the life cycle ideas illustrated here with congregations does apply.

5. 1 Thessalonians 2:1-12.

6. 1 John 2:6.

7. Matthew 6.

8. James 4:13-17.

9. Study Romans 15: 1-17 to see how Paul reminded himself and the church of God's heart for the entire world and how Paul saw worship and ministry as intentionally being priests bringing an offering of Gentiles to God.

10. See 2 Corinthians 1:1-21 for an example of how Paul viewed his ministry as radical dependence on God and the prayers of other believers.

11. Luke 18:8-9.

12. Hebrews 11:6.

13. One example: Luke 16:1-13.

14. Mark 4:1-20

15. Gene Getz. *Sharpening the Image of the Church*

16. Charles Swindoll. *The Bride*

17. Rick Warren. *The Purpose Driven Church*

18. For a full study on the purposes of the Church see Robertson McQuilkin's *Five Smooth Stones: Essential Principles for Biblical Ministry.* Nashville: Broadman & Holman, 2007.

19. Price Pritchett & Ron Pound. *Change: Facing the Problems and Finding the Opportunities.*

20. 1 Thessalonians 1:9-10.

21. Visit www.ciu.edu to find out more about resident and virtual programs at Columbia International University in Columbia, South Carolina.

22. See my book *Life Giving Leadership* for more on the spiritual discipline of lament and grieving.

23. Luke 9:23 is a good principle for God's activity. The encounter with the rich young man who Jesus loved but walked away is a good example.

24. Genesis 2:15.

25. Genesis 3:17.

26. Mark 4:26-29. This parable about the mystery of life within the seed is also used as a foundational principle of Natural Church Development by Christian Schwarz.

27. 1 Corinthians 3:1-10.

28. John 4.

29. 1 Corinthians 3:1-5.

Made in the USA
Middletown, DE
08 June 2017